THE
GLASTON
CANAL

by

GEOFFREY BODY and ROY GALLOP

Ye Olde Cross, Glastonbury.

FROM GLASTONBURY
TO
THE SEA

FIDUCIA PRESS

2001

THE GLASTONBURY CANAL

FROM GLASTONBURY
TO
THE SEA

by

GEOFFREY BODY and ROY GALLOP

Typography   Ken Griffiths

Cover Design   Roy Gallop

Front Cover: Contemporary view of the festivities which attended the opening of the Glastonbury Canal in 1833.

Title Page: Glastonbury's medieval market cross and water conduit survived until a few years before the canal was built.

Rear Cover: The River Brue at Highbridge showing both the clyse and the beginning of the Glastonbury Canal route.

© FIDUCIA PRESS 2001
ISBN 0 946217 08 4
Printed in Great Britain by Doveton Press Ltd., of Bristol

CONTENTS

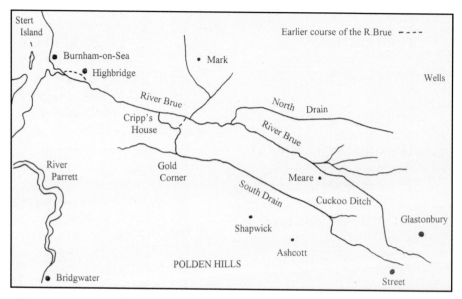

The main waterways of the Brue valley after completion of the works authorized by the 1801 Brue Drainage Act.

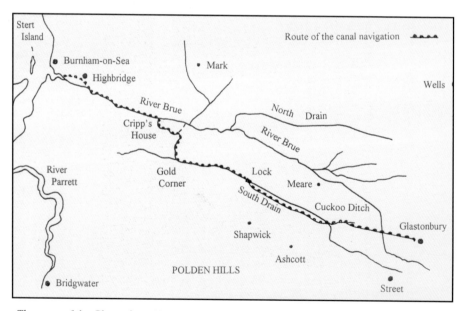

The route of the Glastonbury Navigation & Canal Company's waterway from Glastonbury to the sea at Highbridge.

INTRODUCTION

Glastonbury can be proud of its 19th century canal. Inheriting a water transport tradition going back to Saxon times, the Glastonbury Canal was a local initiative which helped to rescue the town from the economic downturn caused by the loss of its traditional woollen industry to the mills of the North. Getting the canal built demanded a great deal of energy and courage from its dedicated promoters and for a while it brought prosperity back to Glastonbury. That the canal eventually succumbed to mistake, misfortune and the new railway era does not detract from the enterprise and achievements of its builders.

The story of the Glastonbury Canal is a fascinating one. The authors have tried to tell it faithfully and accurately but the surviving records are fragmentary and some of the conclusions drawn from them have had to rely on reason more than on actual records. If any reader is aware of further information we should very much like to be made aware of it via the publishers.

The Old Pump House at Glastonbury, a reminder of the
brief prosperity of its spa in the 18th century.

ORIGINS

*Although the trade of Glastonbury is, at present, but
'the shadow of a shade'; yet a recent plan bids fair to
give the town far greater business, activity and
profitable employment.*   (Rev. Richard Warner)

For hundreds of years the small Somerset settlement at Glastonbury lived in the shadow of its famous abbey. The abbey also controlled large areas throughout the county and the monks undoubtedly made great use of the shallow waterways which were a major feature of the low lying area around Glastonbury itself. These rivers and rhynes were altered and exploited not only for the drainage improvements that would create more land for agricultural purposes but also as a means of conveying the resultant produce to feed the abbey community or for sale in local markets. Not that this was totally new for there is strong evidence of a canal link from the river system to Glastonbury as early as the Saxon period.

In 1539 Glastonbury Abbey was dissolved and its last abbot hanged. A group of Flemish weavers were later accommodated in the old abbey buildings but they did not stay and Glastonbury reverted to leading a very ordinary existence in the midst of a conventional agricultural community. The town was incorporated in 1706 with eight capital burgesses and sixteen inferior burgesses. Wool and cloth were its main concerns until this trade was lost to Northern England. Silk manufacture commenced in Glastonbury around 1793, there was some tanning and fellmongering activity, and agriculture did well as a result of the Napoleonic wars.

Around the middle of the 18th century the Chalice Well spring which once had filled the abbey conduits suddenly regained an age-old reputation for healing. Thousands flocked to take the waters which were reputed to cure illnesses as diverse as leprosy and deafness resulting from naval gunnery. By 1754 the town had its own pumphouse and all the other paraphernalia of a small spa but this activity waned over the years and something else was needed to bring prosperity back to the area.

In the second half of the century the entrepreneurs of Somerset began to take an increasing interest in transport improvements, including the better use of the county's many waterways. Back in 1717 Taunton had started to derive some benefit from the Tone Navigation which brought the town coal from Swansea and heavy goods from Bristol, and by 1769 the route of a Channel to

Channel canal had been surveyed and had included Glastonbury in its plans. Not far away the River Parrett had long carried traffic inland from Bridgwater to Langport and by 1794 there was talk of extending the route further.

The year 1794 was also significant for another, less encouraging, reason. In that year the annual floods proved worse than usual and flood water eventually filled the whole of the Brue valley. The sheer scale of this local disaster prompted action from the Commissioners of Sewers and eventually resulted in the 1801 Brue Drainage Act which gave the river several new channels to improve its flow and added more feeder channels, in particular the North and South Drains. One of the new works was a straight section at Highbridge built south of the meandering original route and another provided a cut-off link east from Cripp's Bridge. Perhaps even more significant were two small local canals which were built in the vicinity of Glastonbury under the umbrella of the 1801 Act and which were designed to provide short links from the River Brue to the peat workings in the North Drain area.

Schemes for ship canals to connect the English and Bristol Channels and avoid the long voyage round Lands End were a regular feature of the years from 1768 to 1870. An offshoot of the resultant activity was the Bridgwater & Taunton Canal which obtained its second Act of Parliament in 1824 and had

Along the Route 1.

The first section of the River Brue which links Highbridge with the sea. Nearest the camera is the new channel opened as a result of the 1801 Brue Drainage Act. The original channel, re-opened as part of the Glastonbury Canal route, began near the moored boats.

opened the 13.5 miles of its Huntworth to Taunton section by 1827. The influential citizens of Glastonbury could not have failed to notice this important improvement to local transport facilities. Coming at a time when the age-old woollen industries had finally been lost to the mills of the North the possibilities offered by improved transport and its ability to provide cheap supplies of coal would have seemed very attractive indeed.

The influences that were to lead to the birth of the Glastonbury Canal were slowly coming together. First was the dwindling of the wool trade from a full-blown industry to a small, individual activity in making worsted stockings. At the same time the heyday of the spa visitors had passed and the town no longer enjoyed their spin-off income. Coupled with this situation the Brue drainage improvements had not fully remedied the annual flood problem. The Commissioners of Sewers were sometimes lacking in enthusiasm for their difficult task, there was a great reluctance to pay the rates they levied, court orders were feeble and monies were always late in payment and inadequate in extent. The land itself, with its high proportion of peat, was hard to drain and the run-off into the existing waterways brought constant silting.

The man who brought all these strands together was Richard Perriam Prat, partner in a Glastonbury law firm. He came from a local family in which the law and the church were strong traditions. Richard was born in 1790 and had grown up aware of the various influences acting upon the town. They would have been in his mind when he became town clerk in 1813 and it needed only a few like-minded people, such as surveyor John Beauchamp of West Pennard, to help him put all the factors together and see a trading waterway as the solution to both the economic and drainage problems of the area.

Richard Prat held a number of important positions in Glastonbury, including Registrar of Births and Deaths, and controlled a significant area of church land. His younger brother Samuel was in business with him and was an Inferior Burgess of the town. Later he was to become clerk to the canal company and treasurer to the South Brue Drain management body. With like-minded associates they called meetings to debate the canal idea and by August 1825 the *Taunton Courier* was reporting on the existence of a firm canal plan to link Glastonbury with the Bristol Channel at Highbridge.

Enough support had been forthcoming to warrant the appointment of a management committee and the commissioning of a route survey in the following year. The man chosen for the survey was Richard Hammett of Street. He would be less expensive than some of the great canal names of the age but he is recorded as a cultivator of heath land and refers to his experience in building a manure canal, possibly one of the two short local waterways built

8

Along the route 2.

Behind the Jubilee Gardens at Highbridge stand these remains of the lock entrance to the canal route. On this side was a tidal wharf at which canal cargoes could be transhipped. On the other, the navigation passed beneath the Bristol turnpike road and rejoined the river.

Along the route 3.

From Highbridge boats and barges for Glastonbury followed the River Brue to Cripp's Corner. There the route turned south along a former channel of the river to resume its west-east course at Gold Corner. Today there are just a few swans on this stretch near Eastern Moor Bridge.

under the 1801 Act. The canal supporters believed they had found the solution to Glastonbury's problems and looked forward eagerly to the results of the Hammett survey.

THE HAMMETT SURVEY

In this instance a great mass of population will be supplied
with almost every necessary, as well as luxury, of life at a
reduced price.   (Prospectus)

The remit to Richard Hammett was 'to take a survey of the level between Glastonbury and Highbridge for the purpose of ascertaining the most eligible line for a water communication between those places'. Two existing waterways were obvious candidates for consideration, the River Brue which already linked the two towns, and the parallel South Drain which had been constructed under the 1801 Act. Hammett examined them both, remarking in his report, 'My first consideration was directed to rendering the River Brue navigable, but I found this measure attended with so many difficulties that I deemed it advisable to adopt some other line.'

One of the main reasons for rejecting the canalisation of the Brue was the key role it played in draining the low lying area west of Glastonbury. This made the river levels hard to predict and control, and the drainage role of the waterway too likely to take precedence over boating considerations. In some parts the winding course of the river would restrict the size of vessel which could be used and altering its profile would be costly. Near Meare Hammett foresaw the need to increase the depth of the river by 3ft over a 3-mile stretch and he expected more problems from an adjoining section where the river ran through blue lias rock for a half mile. The surveyor reckoned that there would need to be a lock on this section to achieve a 7ft rise in the levels and he also warned of the high cost of building bridges and of acquiring riverside land for the towpath.

For all these reasons the surveyor turned his attention to a possible alternative using the South Drain. He walked the prospective course from the River Brue near Cripps's House to Ashcott Corner and then along the ancient Cuckoo Ditch which had connecting links as far as Glastonbury. This, plus the use of the existing river between Cripp's House and Highbridge, led Hammett to comment, 'I was immediately struck with the eligibility of this course.' A consideration that clearly weighed greatly with him was the fact that nearly six miles of this route lay through barren and uncultivated heathland 'where the peat thrown out (in making the waterway deeper and wider) would defray the expenses of cutting.' The South Drain route would also take the proposed canal nearer to the villages along the north side of the Polden Hills.

Having described his preferred route plan, Hammett went on to elaborate on the construction and working detail it entailed. He pointed out that the entrance to the Brue was protected from the worst weather by Stert Island and could already accommodate vessels of up to 200tons burden at all states of the tide. He hit upon the fine idea of using the former channel of the Brue at Highbridge which had been made redundant by the new cut built under the 1801 Act and had only been partially filled in. He planned a floating basin for 250ton vessels to be entered just west of the Highbridge lower flood gates and a lock to connect with the main river above the upper ones. Already capable of handling 20 ton barges, the section from there to Cripp's House would only need the addition of a towpath. The next section on to Cossington Bridge was part of the old course of the Brue and would need little improvement.

For navigation purposes Hammett believed the South Brue Drain would need

Along the route 4

Today Gold Corner is important as one of the control points in the huge and complex task of regulating the drainage and water supply activity throughout the Somerset Levels. It was at Gold Corner that the canal route from Cripp's House met the waters of the main South Drain channel.

to be widened by 4ft to 20ft and be considerably deepened, but he shrewdly remarked that this would benefit the drainage function, clearly a sop for the Commissioners of Sewers whose support for the canal scheme would be needed. He also makes the point that the navigation body would then bear the maintenance cost of the waterway and not the 'frontagers' who had waterside land and who were bound to welcome any relief from the rates levied upon them.

The route via the improved South Drain would take the navigation as far as Mease's Wall, at the western boundary of Meare parish and about seven miles from Highbridge. Here a lock would lift the canal 3ft for the section on to Ashcott Corner where another lock would be needed to achieve a 4ft rise. Hammett mentions that the route 'again touches upon the river Brue' near Glastonbury but presumably saw this as an open connection, possibly to help the canal's water supply. He may have envisaged barges serving Street by using the stretch of the river from the connection point to Pomparles Bridge. According to the survey only seven pieces of land would be cut through in the whole of the canal's making, three of them being needed for the approach to Glastonbury and the building of a basin and wharves there.

Anticipating one of the arguments against his proposals Hammett records:-

It may be objected, that very considerable difficulty will be found in forming a canal through a peat soil, and more particularly in that portion of the line which does not pass through any of the great drains; but from many years' experience I have had in the drainage, management and cultivation of heath lands in this neighbourhood, and from having planned and superintended the cutting of a canal from the north side of the River Brue through a considerable extent of heath ground, for the purpose of conveying manure, I have not the slightest fears as to the practicability of that as well as every other part of the undertaking.

Despite later debates and queries, Hammett's 1826 scheme was imaginative and, indeed, very close to the waterway actually constructed. His biggest mistake was a conclusion that the expenditure would be moderate and not exceed £9,000. However, at the time such a modest figure would, no doubt, have gratified the prime movers in the canal scheme. To go with the Hammett report traffic estimates were being prepared and would go in the prospectus which was now needed to arouse further support.

Along the route 5

At Gold Corner, a lonely spot between Huntspill Moor and Chilton Moor, the north-south direction of the canal navigation again became west-east. Here the channel used to avoid a right angle turn at the junction can be seen merging with the main waterway.

Along the route 6

After using the South Drain for three miles the canal became separate again at the end of Catcott Heath. Shapwick lock was built here at a point known as Mease's (or Maze) Wall and raised vessels by 3ft into the final pound that led them on to Glastonbury.

THE PROSPECTUS

*The promoters of this measure feel great pleasure in
having it in their power to lay before the public a
favourable view of the advantages which may be
expected from it.* (Prospectus)

The prospectus issued to solicit support for the scheme for a canal from
Glastonbury to Highbridge began by setting out Richard Hammett's survey in
full and then provided details of the traffic which might be expected to pass
along the waterway. As a preamble to the information on anticipated tonnages
of specific commodities the promoters described the population catchment
area as one of 55,000 people. They stated that the towns and villages involved
were currently dependent on costly land carriage from the ports of Bristol,
Bridgwater, Weymouth and Bridport for the supply of 'almost all the neces-
saries, as well as the luxuries, of life'. They declared:-

*Glastonbury lies nearly in the centre of this highly populous and productive
country, and within a much shorter distance of these different towns and villages (with which it communicates by excellent roads) than the above mentioned ports; it may therefore be fairly presumed that from Glastonbury all
their supplies would be drawn (i.e. after being carried on the proposed canal).*

The Rev. Richard Warner's contemporary book *The History of Glastonbury*
contains extensive reference to the canal scheme and makes it clear that the
promoters expected to serve a significant inland area east of Glastonbury, the
towns of Shepton Mallet, Bruton, Wincanton, Sherborne, Yeovil and Milborne
Port being mentioned in addition to Wells and Glastonbury. A strong point
was also made in this work of the drainage benefits the canal would bring to
'a tract of country particularly barren and unproductive'.

After the general observations the prospectus turned to specific flows of
potential traffic, dealing with the inwards movements to Glastonbury first.
Based upon a population which was 'daily increasing', demand was expected
for significant movements of building materials listed thus:-

*Of deals alone there will be annually carried on the canal to
Glastonbury.....* *3000 tons*

Of iron...... *1000 tons*

Of slate.....	*600 tons*
Of tiles and bricks.....	*2500 tons*

According to the subtext the softwood boards known as deals were proving difficult to obtain locally, partly due to the 'heavy expense of land-carriage' from the importing ports. The carriage cost was confidently expected to decrease when the canal was opened but if the increasing use of elm as a substitute continued the canal promoters expected it to 'find a ready market' as pit props 'in the mining districts of Wales.' In connection with the tile and brick estimates, the prospectus referred to the high quality and reasonable price of such items manufactured at Highbridge and along the River Parrett.

Among the more general inwards cargoes it was expected that some of the goods produced in the Midlands factories and shipped down the River Severn would pass along the canal to the benefit of Glastonbury. Salt movements were expected to be substantial in view of the extent of dairy farming around Glastonbury and mention was made of 'one house at Shepton Mallet' which

Along the route 7

At Ashcott Corner the South Drain turned away from its west-east course but the canal route continued ahead. This meant that the canal route had to cross the drainage channel and did so by means of a small aqueduct of which the stonework remains can still be seen here.

produced some 500 tons of salt annually from rock which had to be carried by horse transport over the 24 miles from Bridgwater. The general cargo tonnages were estimated as:-

Of slate.....	*600 tons*
Of salt and salt rock.....	*1000 tons*
Of hides, bark, groceries, Birmingham and Sheffield articles, and hoops, hurdles and staves.....	*700 tons*
Of wheat.....	*300 tons*

The prospectus then moved on to the question of coal movement, the most vital of the traffic flows expected. The traditional pattern had been for the Glastonbury area to obtain its supplies from 'the Mendip collieries' which would have involved carriage by cart or pack horse from the Radstock area and over the top of the Mendip range. The slow journey would incur turnpike tolls, take a considerable time and be quite expensive. In contrast the settlements which had access to one of the ports or pills along the Somerset coastline received their coal direct from Wales or the Forest of Dean, shipped in quantity in ketches and trows and more moderately priced as a result. From these tiny harbours coal was delivered around the area in farm carts or collected by those with transport. The diaries of Parson Holland of Nether Stowey, for example, record in 1804 'Captain Davis called this day informing us of coal at Combych.' Cheap coal was the key to commercial prosperity but, although they did mention coal used for lime burning, the canal promoters based their traffic estimates on 14,000 people each using a ton of coal a year. They recorded:-

the import would be 14,000 tons; but, in order to avoid any thing like an excessive calculation, we will deduct 8,000 tons.....	*6000 tons*

The prospectus next turned its attention to traffic outwards from the Glastonbury area, floating the idea that the stone traffic alone would be enough to make the canal viable. Reference was made to 'inexhaustible quarries in the parishes of Walton, Street, Butleigh and Keinton' and to the high quality of the paving stone they produced. Keen to continue the element of

Along the route 8

East of Ashcott Corner the canal route and its railway successor changed sides. In this illustration the probable line of the canal lies between the line of the former railway trackbed on the right and the minor drainage ditch on the left and is marked by the central trees.

Along the route 9

On its approach to Glastonbury the canal crossed the River Brue by means of a three-arched viaduct with a siphon beneath. Surviving viaduct masonry is pictured here with the Brue in the foreground and evidence of the canal and railway routes to Glastonbury beyond.

caution in the tonnage estimates it was pointed out that such stone was already being distributed to points twenty to thirty miles distant making it a prime prospect for transfer to the canal. The text concluded:-

we will assume that there pass annually on the canal only.....	*2000 tons*
Of elm and oak timber.....	*1000 tons*
Of beans, barley and malt.....	*600 tons*
Of cyder and cheese.....	*200 tons*

Totalling up all this tonnage the prospectus applied a theoretical rate of a penny per ton per mile to the 18,900 tons involved, assumed it would all pass over the full 13 miles of the canal and calculated the annual receipts to be £1023 . 15s. A further calculation was then made for the charges to levied on vessels entering the floating basin. For this a rate of a penny per ton was applied to the 12,900 ton proportion of inwards traffic that would be seaborne and to the 15,000 tons of coal which was considered likely to arrive for domestic consumers in the Highbridge area. This added £116 . 5s to the anticipated receipts and brought the total annual earnings up to £1,140.

After stating that their 'calculations will unquestionably bear a comparison with any others taken for a similar purpose' the compilers of the document went on to deal with the costs likely to be incurred in running the canal asserting that 'the annual expense upon the line must be very inconsiderable. ' If only they had known!

The promoters' assumption was that short distance traffic would earn more than enough to cover the costs of running the undertaking. They averred that:-

The canal passing through the heath lands, great quantities of manure would be conveyed both up and down for the purpose of improving them.

The peat which is cut for fuel, and which is taken to the distance of 20, and even 30 miles, would, by means of the canal, be brought out of the heath which is intersected but by two stoned roads, in a line of nearly, or quite, 6 miles.

Corn, which is grown in great abundance on and near Poldon-hill and

Hunstpill, and almost wholly sold to millers resident at Glastonbury, Wells and their vicinity, would be put in barges at the point where the road from Edington to Mark crosses the canal, and at Highbridge, and be thus conveyed to Glastonbury, thereby saving a land carriage of at least 10 miles.

Building and paving stone, from Street, would also be taken in large quanti-ties for the supply of Meare, Wedmore, and other places adjacent.

The canal promoters also referred to the proposals to link the Bristol and English Channels by a ship canal and saw this as a further prospect, especial-ly for moving paving stone to the areas through which that canal might pass. After this final observation on traffic prospects they moved on to their con-clusions, recording:-

The calculations of the probable profit to the subscribers having been so fully, and, it is hoped, satisfactorily gone into, little is requisite to be added as to the benefits likely to accrue to the public; it being clear, that a measure of this nature can never be profitable to the proprietors without being of utility to the

Along the route 10

The canal approach to Glastonbury entailed an awkward right hand bend where the route turned sharply to run alongside Dyehouse Lane and the Mill Stream. All that now remains to identify this spot is a curve in the boundary fence and a few odd pieces of masonry.

public at large. In this instance a great mass of population will be supplied with almost every necessary, as well as luxury, of life, at a reduced price; an extensive market will be opened for the products of the country round; and a barren and uncultivated waste, of at least 5,000 acres, will, in a few years, become highly productive land. This latter consideration alone would entitle the measure to general approbation; but, as every other circumstances is so entirely favourable to the undertaking, the promoters most confidently submit it to the public, fully convinced that it will meet with the liberal support which they conceive it so justly merits.

In conclusion they cannot but observe, that their object has not been to get up a scheme that shall be profitable to the few; but, on the contrary, by taking the shares at £25 each, to allow even the humblest individual to become a sub-scriber, and thereby a participator in the profits so fairly expected to arise from this small but important work.

As a footnote to this latter point it was recorded that the deposit on each share at the time of subscription was to be £2. As construction was expected to take two or three years the calls for further cash would be well spread out and thus no burden to those with only modest sums to invest.

This prospectus, as far as it went, seemed a very reasonable document. The route made sense and the traffic flows were fairly down to earth. The weakness lay in its reliance on Hammett's figure of £9,000 for the capital cost without any details of the specific costs of acquiring land or the requirements and methods of construction. On a capital outlay of £9,000 an annual return of £1,140 was reasonable, but the true cost figure was to be considerably higher than this estimate.

AN ACT IS OBTAINED

An Act for improving and supporting the Navigation of the
River Brue from the Mouth thereof, at its Junction with
the River Parrett, to Cripp's House, and for making and
constructing a Canal from thence to the Town of
Glastonbury in the County of Somerset.

(7-8 Geo.IV - Sess. 1826-7)

With the route surveyed and the potential traffic assessed the promoters of the Glastonbury Canal lost no time in setting about the tasks of lobbying support, raising money and preparing their approach to Parliament. Somewhere along the way the Hammett survey was challenged and John Beauchamp Jnr of West Pennard, another local surveyor, undertook to re-examine Hammett's conclusions. Following his own survey of the route Beauchamp concluded that the canal could operate at one level throughout and needed only stop locks to prevent its waters flowing to or from the Brue and the Mill Stream at the Glastonbury end. His reasoning was probably that the depth of water required to eliminate lock rises could be obtained by holding back a sufficient volume of fresh water by means of suitable gates at Highbridge. His cost

Along the route 11

Glastonbury no longer has a railway station but the site is marked by a pair of gates in the old
level crossing style. The canal route terminated here in a small basin which lay roughly in the
centre of the scene depicted and which was replaced by the passenger station and goods yard

estimate was a more realistic £15,234.

By the beginning of 1827 the capital requirement estimate had increased to £18,000 to allow for such things as Parliamentary expenses and changes in the specification, but at least enthusiasm for the scheme was high and it was making significant progress. Subscriptions were clearly not a problem at this stage as the *Taunton Courier* was able to report in its issue of 28 February 1827:-

Monday week a highly respectable meeting was held at the Town Hall, Glastonbury for the purpose of informing the subscribers of the progress already made in forwarding this most important work. The Mayor having taken the chair, it was stated by Mr S.Pratt that all landed proprietors had given their consent to the undertaking, and that the estimate of the work was 18,000l, 4,000l of which only remained to be prescribed, and he had no doubt, when the advantages likely to result from the canal were fully known, the remaining sum would soon be made up.

It was further stated by Mr Pratt that the population within 10 miles around the intended line of the canal amounted to 50,000 and no fewer than 70,000 persons would be benefited by the completion of the work. Mr E.T.Percy, The Engineer, also addressed the meeting in favour of the project, and the greatest unanimity appearing to pervade the assembly there is no doubt that applications will forthwith be made to Parliament for a bill to carry this vast and important design into full effect.

It is not known what Mr Percy's qualifications and status were but more general matters continued to go well. The subscriptions rose to £15,250 and by 30 May 1827 the same newspaper was reporting on further success:-

We are informed that the Bill for carrying into effect the objects of the promoters of this undertaking has passed through both houses of Parliament and received the Royal Assent. Great rejoicings have been manifested at Glastonbury and its neighbourhood.

The plans which accompanied the Act of Parliament show a route identical to that in the Hammett survey. The Glastonbury Navigation & Canal Company, as the undertaking was called, was empowered to purchase land and construct its waterway from a straightened section of the old route of the Brue at Highbridge and then along the river to Broad Warth and Cripp's Bridge where the line turned south to meet the South Drain. This was then used to Ashcott Corner where the route continued along the Cuckoo Ditch before the final section into Glastonbury and 'a proper and convenient basin' near the Mill Stream.

The Act listed the first proprietors of the new undertaking as:-

Charles Browne esquire, George Bond, John Beauchamp senior, John Bulleid, John Henry Burgess, Richard Chapman, Joseph Clarke, Cornish,* William Dyke, Robert Giles, Sir Alexander Hood, baronet, Elizabeth Hood, John Holman, Henry Hodge, esquire, Thomas Lawrence, Aaron Moody, esquire, Thomas Maddison, Thomas Moore, Eleanor Talbott Moore, Robert Moore, Jonathan Payne Newman, William Benjamin Naish, William Parfitt, Richard Panter, Henry Penny, Thomas Roach, esquire, William Reeves, James Rood, George Rich, esquire, Peter Davis Sherston, esquire, John Smith, John Tucker, Bartholomew Wake, Thomas Guy Wake, Lockyear Walton and William Vale. *

It has not been possible to identify the forename of Mr. Cornish.

Although the Prat brothers were the solicitors for the canal company they do

Highbridge Sluice today, a location that once caused so much conflict between the canal and drainage interests.

not appear in the Act's list of proprietors. However, several of their known associates do, and a Miss Ann Prat contributed £2,000 of the £18,000 capital authorized by the Act. The latter sum was to be made up of 360 shares of £50 each and there were borrowing powers for a further £5,000 which would be secured by mortgage. The whole of the £18,000 had to be raised before the Act became operative.

John Beauchamp's father was one of the proprietors, Browne and Reeves were local bankers, Bond and Burgess doctors and Bulleid, Naish and Rood were Inferior Burgesses of the town. The remainder of the proprietors of the Glastonbury Navigation & Canal Company, whose seal was based on the Glastonbury coat of arms and a Severn Trow, were mainly local people of some standing in the community. Bulleid, Bond and Chapman subscribed £3,200 between them and a J.J.Roach took shares to the value of £1,500. Some of these people may have been Prat nominees or the Prats may have made good the subscription shortfall. The scheme also had the support of Welsh coal interests, a senior figure in the Monmouthshire Canal company subscribing £350.

The Act gave the canal company the right to acquire the land it needed subject to a specified procedure. It was authorized to charge up to 1/6d per ton for non-perishable traffics such as 'coals, culm, coke, cinders, charcoal, timber, iron, bricks, tiles, stone, slate, turf and manure'. Since the length of the new waterway was quoted as 14 miles, 1 furlong, 7 chains, this rate is slightly above the prospectus figure of 1d per ton per mile. A higher figure of 3/- per ton was stipulated for higher value traffics such as 'cheese, timber and other goods, wares, merchandise and commodities,' i.e. for general merchandise. For goods on hand more than 24 hours the company could fix wharfage charges of up to 3d per ton for periods of less than six days.

Duties laid upon the canal company in the Act included erecting a new bridge to carry the Bristol road over the waterway at Highbridge and a tide lock there with two sea doors and a freshwater door. It was required to construct a towpath and to provide a number of bridges to maintain land access. In view of what happened later the directive to ensure the canal was watertight by ensuring the bottom and sides were well puddled is also interesting.

Not surprisingly drainage considerations feature prominently in the Glastonbury Canal Act. It protected the rights of the Commissioners of Sewers and forbade the canal company to obstruct or hinder the drainage process. The Highbridge tide sluice, which was critical to the release of water from the land side into the Parrett, was specifically protected, another feature which foreshadowed future events. In recognition of the position of the

Commissioners the canal company was required to find another £1,000 and deposit it with drainage authority nominees as a surety against any costs the latter might incur as a result of the construction of the canal.

The 87 pages of the Act embraced a great number of other provisions, many of them fairly standard to the canal Acts which had been passed since the Canal Mania years. Landowners' rights were protected, a procedure laid down for land acquisition, access rights and navigation procedures defined and penalties stipulated to discourage interference or damage. Among the water management clauses was one requiring the waters of the Brue and the Mill Stream to be safeguarded and the canal company also had to 'save harmless' the lands on which the South Drain rates were levied. The whole document was accompanied by plans showing the impact of the new waterway on each parish through which it passed.

CONSTRUCTION

On one stretch near Burtle no bottoming was done
at all. This was said to be due to 'an unfortunate
event which occurred during the performance of
the work.'
(The Glastonbury Canal, Dr A.M.Boyd)

With so few records of the canal undertaking surviving the exact sequence of events which followed the passing of the canal company's Act in 1827 has to be partly conjectural. The first stage was undoubtedly the formal conclusion of the various land purchase deals with attention then turning to preparation for the physical works which had to be undertaken. Broadly these fell into four distinct categories viz the major works at Highbridge, new canal construction from Maze Lock to Glastonbury, widening and deepening elsewhere, and the towpath, lock, aqueducts, and bridges along the route.

Quite early in the proceedings grave doubts were raised about the adequacy and accuracy of the previous surveys. These appear to have arisen soon after construction commenced and may have been compounded by limited experience of the specialist work involved in building canals. Whatever the catalyst, the proprietors quickly called in an expert for a further opinion. The man they chose for the task was John Rennie, son of a famous canal engineer father.

Rennie examined the Glastonbury Canal project and came up with three possibilities. One was to provide a depth of 10ft throughout the waterway to make it capable of accepting large vessels all the way up to Glastonbury. Such a depth would have been sufficient for large sloops and small brigs of up to 140 tons which was well above the average size of local Bristol Channel shipping and would have accommodated coasting vessels from Ireland and even the Continent. This option was estimated to cost £38,250 and was way beyond the promoters' means. At the other end of the scale Rennie considered confining the waterway to 5ft wide barges which would have meant that all traffic would have needed transhipment at Highbridge. This was costed at £22,850 but would have imposed serious restrictions on the canal proprietors' ambitions for their undertaking.

The other option, and the one Rennie recommended, was for an 8ft deep waterway which would accommodate the 40-60 ton trows and ketches which were the norm for coal movements from Wales, vessels carrying goods transhipped at Bristol and other local shipping movements. He saw no need to amend the basic route of the waterway but recommended that the top section should be altered into an independent pound fed by water from the Mill Stream but with its course kept separate from that flow. This pound would also separate from the South Drain on the eastern side of Westhay Heath by

At Ashcott Corner the South Drain turns away from the canal route amid the peat which caused the latter so many problems.

means of a lock at Maze (or Mease's) Wall which would provide a rise of 3ft 2ins and avoid the drawbacks of Beauchamp's plan to pen back water as a way of overcoming the route gradient. This lock and the one at Highbridge were to be 64ft long and 18ft wide.

Rennie further proposed the replacement of the two Brue locks by an aqueduct to carry the canal over the River Brue and a siphon to pass its waters beneath. This 18ft wide, 3-arch structure was to have a smaller, single-arch companion over the South Drain at Ashcott Corner. The standard section of the canal was to be 20ft wide at the bottom and 44ft wide at the top and the sharp curve on the approach to Glastonbury ought, said Rennie, to be eased. He calculated that the cost of all this would be £28,720.

Despite this cost escalation the proprietors now had a much firmer plan for the canal works. Activity resumed after Rennie's recommendations of July 1828 were adopted. He provided specifications for the main civil engineering features of the scheme and no doubt gave the canal engineer some general advice on good construction practices. Rennie remained associated with the project until well into 1829 and seems to have added further changes to the original ones. Partly to save money the position of the Highbridge sea lock

An eighteenth century etching showing canal and river navigation. Wind power, horse power, and man power are evident in this picture as methods of propulsion.

was moved to an upper site near the bridge which meant that the wharf built along the downstream section would be tidal. At some period the plan to ease the sharp approach bend at Glastonbury was dropped, possibly because it would have meant acquiring extra land to permit a gentler curvature.

In July 1830 the Commissioners of Sewers appointed I.M.Tucker to report on 'the works done or omitted to be done by the Glastonbury Canal Company.' In the following month Tucker began this task by inspecting the two aqueducts in company with Samuel Prat, a canal director named Emery and a Mr Allen who was described as the Superintendent of the Works for the canal company. At the end of 1830 Tucker heard that there were irregularities with the construction work at Highbridge and found this to be true in respect of excavations to the west of the turnpike road. He and Allen reached a compromise, Tucker reporting that:-

in the then disturbed state of the Country it was thought better that the work should be allowed to proceed under certain regulations which we made than to stop it and turn the men loose on the country.

At this period there was a growing demand for reform following the second French Revolution and the first signs of later extensive rioting were manifesting themselves. By February 1831 Tucker again had to visit the Highbridge site and reported, 'I found that the contractor had run away and the work at a stand still.' Another contractor must have been found for more dialogue was required about the Highbridge work later that year, Tucker then turning his attention to the aqueducts in 1832.

The scarcity of canal records is partly relieved by the existence of a report from the directors of the Glastonbury Canal to its subscribers dated 21 December 1831. It is probably more optimistic than the circumstances warranted but it does provide some useful factual information on the project at that point. Apparently due to the effect of the depression on its agricultural supporters only £12,500 of the original subscriptions had been forthcoming and even then a few of the main subscribers had needed 'to take up all the doubtful shares' in order to avoid a fall in their trading value. To date £40 of each £50 share had been 'called' and further £5 calls were scheduled for January and April 1832.

Agreement had been reached with the Exchequer Bill Loan Commissioners based on completion affidavits from the contractors and providing for a £5,000 loan over twenty years at a rate of 5%. This plus the remaining calls would, it was said, enable completion. The traffic estimate in the report had risen to 50,000 tons which would yield £2,500 annually to provide £500 for working expenses, £250 for loan repayment and £250 for redemption of capital, leaving £1,500 as the return on the £13,000 capital outlay.

The canal specification was confirmed as 10ft deep and 45ft wide to Maze's Wall and 7ft deep x 35ft wide on to Glastonbury. The directors made the point that the dimensions of the lock - 64ft long x 18ft wide x 10ft deep - demonstrated their confidence in the project and would enable them to take 200ton vessels into Highbridge and those up to 70tons beyond. Provision had been made for making the top section 45ft x 10ft if necessary and a progress report on the main works showed the aqueduct ready apart from its top plate and that water had already been let into the lock. Some settling of banks and masonry was still required but the works generally were said to be 'very forward and proceeding rapidly.'

The cast iron aqueduct across the River Brue was built by Glastonbury blacksmith John Wright who later revealed that it had cost nearly £3,000. It seems likely that the other main works must have cost similar amounts so that with the addition of widening, puddling, bridging, towpaths and the like the available cash had been quickly consumed and only the loan and the extra contributions from a faithful few had enabled the enterprise to continue. A combination of reading between the lines and events that were to happen later raises the strong implication that stringent economies were practised wherever possible and may even have affected the standard of the works, especially the adequacy of the clay lining of the waterway. One report even suggests that along one stretch near Burtle no bottoming was provided at all. Additionally, poor Rennie got only £200 towards his bill of £567 and money became so tight that the Commissioners of Sewers had to sue the canal company in 1831 for non-payment of the £1,000 that was supposed to be lodged with them.

Like so many of its predecessors the Glastonbury Canal was having a hard time. It was costing much more than anticipated and many of its subscribers had regretted their original optimism. At the same time to abandon the undertaking would be to lose all the money already invested. There was no choice but to continue, to make further calls upon the subscribers and to watch every penny of expenditure with an eagle eye. Eventually the construction was brought to near completion and the proprietors could at last begin to hope that their bright traffic expectations would be realised and a long awaited dividend on their investment might be forthcoming.

This illustration of the triumphant cavalcade returning to Glastonbury on the canal opening day shows both guests and onlookers still in the highest of spirits.

OPEN AT LAST

This great and useful undertaking having been
completed, was opened on the 15th ultimo early
in the morning, the road leading from the town
to the basin was thronged with spectators.
(Bridgwater & Somersetshire General Advertiser)

Thus began a contemporary account in a newspaper dated 2 September 1833. All the problems which the Glastonbury Navigation & Canal had encountered during the lengthy construction period seemed to have been surmounted. At last the promoters' early dreams had been translated into a fine waterway route from the Somerset coast at Highbridge to the historic town of Glastonbury. The mood was one of great rejoicing. As the newspaper put it, 'the whole population appeared to be on the qui vive.'

The opening day celebrations took place on 15 August 1833. The main event was a waterway cavalcade from Glastonbury to Highbridge and back. It set off from Glastonbury about 7am watched by a considerable crowd around the canal basin on the edge of town. A band played stirring music and the bells of the town's churches rang out a 'merry peal.' The boats got back to Glastonbury about six in the evening to more cheering and the waving of top hats by the spectators on the towpath.

Pride of place in the cavalcade went to the canal company's barge which they had named *Goodland* and to a 'beautiful yacht', the *Water Witch*. These were followed by at least two official barges, one containing guests drinking a toast to the enterprise, and the other the fourteen or so musicians of the official band. There are indications that the canal company did acquire two 45ton barges at some stage and these may well have been the ones. Most of the boats were towed by teams of three sailors but several private rowing boats and small yachts also joined in the procession. Towing took place on both banks and a buxom pie seller offered her wares to the animated crowd which lined them.

Nine days later the canal company arranged another celebration, this time principally for 'the respectable trading classes'. The bells again rang out, this time backed up by a little cannon fire, and the band again put in an appearance. To liven up the event an element of competition was introduced between the *Goodland* and a new yacht belonging to J.Vincent and called *St Vincent*. No doubt the yacht would have used a little sail if the wind was right but towing must again have been the main form of propulsion. Whatever it was, the *Goodland* got to Highbridge an hour before its rival and doubtless indulged in some good natured banter with the guests on the laggard yacht when it did arrive. The whole outing was probably in the nature of 'sea trials' for the brand new *St Vincent* which sprang a leak on the return journey. Fortunately the *Goodland* was able to turn back and render assistance and the evening return to Glastonbury was completed without further incident.

Concluding its report on the canal opening celebrations the *Bridgwater & Somersetshire General Advertiser* said 'We understand it is the intention of a large party of gentlemen of Glastonbury, shortly to give a public dinner, in a commodious booth, to be erected near the aqueduct in the vicinity of town'.

The Glastonbury Canal was now open for traffic. Not only had the physical works been completed but the company had set up an administrative system conforming to its enabling Act and designed to serve the dual objective of controlling traffic operations and collecting and accounting for revenue. In overall strategic control there was a Committee of Directors, chosen from those holding at least four shares and serving for one year. For more practical day-to-day control the company was empowered to appoint a Treasurer and Clerk or to combine these roles in one person. This was the post that Samuel Prat occupied.

For the actual operation of the enterprise the company had collectors at each end of the route to collect the tolls, wharfage and other charges due. Tolls had to be exhibited and masters of each vessel were required to give an account of their cargo to these collectors at Highbridge or Glastonbury and to detail any goods that had been discharged on their journey, a provision designed to ensure charges were levied on any intermediate cargoes. Masters had to navigate with care and pay for any damage they did. If a vessel sank it had to be removed quickly and all boats had to have their name painted on the outside. The bargees themselves were forbidden to use nets or guns in pursuit of extra game for their home cooking pot!

Water control was also important. The Act had protected the supplies of fresh water in the canal area and made provision for ensuring the users of water from the Brue and the Mill Stream were not disadvantaged. These intentions had to be honoured in practice if the canal company was not to be harassed by angry mill owners and others who depended upon water for their livelihood or livestock. To ensure equitable passage along the waterway lock keepers were strictly enjoined to afford no undue preference to one vessel over another.

In its early years the canal appears to have been quite successful. A little over a year after opening the *Sherborne Journal* was reporting an increase in local building in Glastonbury and recording that 'timber, slate, coal, salt, iron and all articles of general consumption are imported in abundance, and at very reduced prices, through the canal.' The newspaper judged the canal as being 'of great utility' and likely to provide 'a very handsome return' for its investors.

By 1836 the Reverend W. Phelps was also saying in *The History and Antiquities of Somerset* that the trade in these basic commodities was increasing. He makes another, highly revealing comment, viz:-

Another important advantage to the marsh country is that the flood waters now pass off rapidly through the lock-gates of the canal, which are opened when the water is high, and a double outlet is made in addition to the original sluices; thereby relieving the marsh of its waters, in about as many days as it required weeks heretofore.

An 1840 directory observed that, 'The canal that has lately connected the town with the river Parrett has tended much to advance its prosperity' and recorded three substantial commercial users at the Glastonbury end, viz:-

Roy Gallop

There was probably some local use of the canal and its connecting waterways based on traditional craft like this one.

John Underwood (lime burner), Canal Wharf.
J.N.Best & Co (merchants, wharfingers, timber, deal, slate), Canal Head.
Stuckey & Bagehot, Canal Head.

The canal company had two 45-ton barges of its own which had originally been designed for carrying peat in the Meare area. Traffic transhipped at Bridgwater or Highbridge seems to have moved in smaller vessels of about 25 tons with the remainder conveyed by sea-going trows that passed through the sea lock, lowered their masts to pass beneath the two bridges and then used wind, tide or towage to complete their journey. No doubt there was some small boat use of the canal for passengers and local freight but it is unlikely to have been of significant volume.

Although all seemed to be going well, in fact bad times lay ahead. However, the canal seems to have enjoyed five or more years of successful operation and it is interesting to note that at least two schemes were mooted for connecting railways, as envisaged in the enabling Act. One of these was for a railroad from Glastonbury Wharf to Yeovil, Sherborne and Dorsetshire and the other for a 'Railroad from Glastonbury Canal Co Wharf near St Benedict's Bridge, Glastonbury to West End Bruton, with a branch line to Wincanton.'

TROUBLED TIMES

The principal cause of their failure is attributed to
the unprosperous state of the Glastonbury Canal
(Taunton Courier)

Whatever the chroniclers might say about the early years of the Glastonbury Canal enterprise it seems clear that the levels of traffic it was carrying were quite insufficient to service the capital consumed in setting up the enterprise. There were problems too in maintaining the water level in the canal and these, in turn, created difficulties for potential shippers and thus made the basic problem worse. In 1840 matters were to come to a head in dramatic fashion with the failure of the firm which had taken a leading role in the whole of the canal's affairs.

In the first month of 1840 the Prat brothers disappeared leaving behind them financial chaos that was to spell ruin for many of their clients. There is little doubt that the Prat family had put up the extra money demanded by the rising estimates and construction costs of the canal and it is highly likely that some of this came from money placed with their legal firm for investment. After all, this firm was highly respected, Richard was town clerk and the canal scheme was supposed to be making everyone's fortune. Clearly the reverse was the case and when the brothers fled they left behind them a financial shortfall estimated at £40,000 to £50,000. The Prat brothers were declared bankrupt and their effects were sold off. Richard was removed from the office of town clerk and from his position as churchwarden and as a Commissioner of Sewers and eventually surfaced again in America.

The drama of the Prats' flight was heightened by the suicide of another canal shareholder, John Bulleid. He had acted as guarantor for some of the Prat bonds and had been unable to meet his financial commitments partly because his canal shares had shrunk in value and produced little in the way of dividends. In dramatic fashion he put an end to his problems by leaping from the tower of St John's Church, Glastonbury.

Although the canal had seemed to fulfil its proprietors' expectations in terms of land drainage in the early years, insidious factors had been at work and slowly reversed this position. The initial difficulties stemmed from the fact that the water level in the upper pound between Shapwick Lock and Glastonbury was so high that it inhibited drainage from the fields and moors around. Along this section the adjoining land was mostly peat which soon became so swollen with the retained rainfall that the whole surface rose several feet. In turn this lifted the bottom of the canal and fractured it in those places where the clay puddling had been less than thorough. Water seeped out adding to the waterlogging of the surrounding land and reducing the depth available for navigation.

To the consternation of water users along the Brue and the Mill Stream their waters were diverted into the canal to improve the depth available for navigation, but this was no long term solution. Soon the larger trows could no longer make the through journey from Highbridge to Glastonbury with any degree of confidence and more and more of the cargoes had to be transhipped at the former point. This, of course, added to the cost of using the canal and reduced its competitive edge over alternative means of movement.

And there were other changes too. Even as the canal had opened influential merchants in Bristol had been talking about a railway line from that city to Exeter. The Bristol & Exeter Railway issued its prospectus in 1835 and by 1841 was ready to open the section from Bristol to Bridgwater. This stretch, through Highbridge, duly opened on 14 June 1841 to be followed by exten-

ANNO UNDECIMO & DUODECIMO

VICTORIÆ REGINÆ.

****

Cap. xxviii.

An Act for enabling the *Bristol and Exeter* Railway Company to purchase the *Glastonbury* Navigation and Canal, and for amending the Acts relating to such Railway and Canal.

[30th *June* 1848.]

WHEREAS an Act was passed in the Sixth Year of the Reign of His late Majesty King *William* the Fourth, intituled *An Act for making a Railway from* Bristol *to* Exeter, *with Branches to the Towns of* Bridgewater *in the County of* Somerset *and* Tiverton *in the County of* Devon : And whereas several other Acts were passed in the First, in the Third, in the Fourth and Fifth, in the Eighth and Ninth, and in the Ninth and Tenth Years of the Reign of Her present Majesty, relating to the *Bristol and Exeter* Railway, and for authorizing the Construction of certain Branches therefrom : And whereas another Act was passed in the Eighth Year of the Reign of His Majesty King *George* the Fourth, intituled *An Act for improving and supporting the Navigation of the River* Brue, *from the Mouth thereof, at its Junction with the River* Parrett, *to* Cripps's House, *and for making and constructing a Canal from thence to the Town of* Glastonbury *in the County of* Somerset : And whereas the said *Glastonbury* Navigation and Canal might be more economically and beneficially worked in connexion with the Railways and

6 & 7 W. 4. c. 36.

7 & 8 G. 4. c. 41.

[*Local.*]   4 *C*   Works

36

sion to Taunton in 1842, to Wellington (Beam Bridge) in 1843 and to Exeter in 1844. About the same time as the new railway reached Highbridge the latter also got a new turnpike road to Wells. Both may have brought some extra business for the canal, for it was still carrying regular traffic in 1844, but by now the enterprise made poor comparison with the high hopes of the promotion years.

The B&E railway had had to sacrifice some planned branches in order to finance its main line but now this was open the company began to look for feeder routes. At the same time the 1845 agreement on competition between the Great Western and London & South Western railways had broken down and the latter was actively seeking expansion into the West Country. Seeing the canal as a possible feeder route, to head-off possible L&SW infiltration and for the waterway's land value, the Bristol & Exeter Railway sent its company secretary to Glastonbury late in 1846 to discuss the possibility of purchase.

A deal between the railway and canal companies was concluded in the middle of 1847. The price eventually agreed was £7,000 which showed how low the value of the waterway had sunk. But other local navigations were already suffering from railway competition and its water problems were getting no easier so the proprietors of the Glastonbury Canal were only too glad to sell.

Some of the B&E shareholders had reservations about the purchase and expressed these at a meeting in May 1848. One speaker said he had been to the canal time after time but 'had never seen a boat in his life'. Another had heard that a mortgage on the canal had once been sold for half its face value making the proposed purchase price of £7,000 far too much. The chairman had to admit that the canal was only earning £300 a year but was confident that this could be turned into a profit. His hint that others were interested in the waterway suggested a hidden agenda behind the railway actions.

The upshot of the negotiations and deliberations was a firm agreement for the purchase of the canal and this was duly reflected in an Act of Parliament - the Bristol & Exeter Railway (Glastonbury Navigation & Canal Purchase) Act - which received the Royal Assent on 30 June 1848. The Act was for 'enabling the Bristol & Exeter Railway to purchase the Glastonbury Navigation & Canal' and recorded the belief that the canal 'might be more economically and beneficially worked in connexion with the Railway and Works' of the B&E company.

The luckless canal shareholders were going to get back a final total of £7,372, less than half their original outlay, and the waterway that had been their pride and joy was so silted up that it was earning only a quarter of the revenue anticipated in the prospectus. At a rate of 1/6d per ton the £300 earnings figure equates to an annual tonnage of around 4,000 tons and something like three barge loads a week. Hardly a thriving business.

END OF THE LINE

To relinquish the maintenance of the said Navigation
and Canal as a Navigation, and to authorize the
appropriation of the same for the purpose of constructing
the said Railway.   (Notice in the Bridgwater Times)

Although the Bristol & Exeter Railway had agreed to purchase the Glastonbury Canal and secured an enabling Act in 1848 for that purpose, the formalities took some time to complete. A letter of 13th November 1849 confirms that a special B&E meeting had approved the purchase but indicates that conveyancing was still in progress. Another records on 25 November 1850 that the 'purchase of the canal (was) only just completed.' In fact the bond which the B&E had to provide for the Commissioners of Sewers to replace the one originally furnished by the canal company was not lodged with the Commissioners until August 1851.

It also took until 1851 before the affairs of the original canal company were wound up and its unfortunate shareholders received the balance of the purchase price after outstanding debts had been paid. During this time the railway had clearly been running the navigation but the old cosy relationship between the canal and the Commissioners, which had been helped by the fact that many of the latter were canal proprietors, began to crumble. As early as January 1848 a body of six Commissioners had appointed themselves as watchdogs in connection with the canal sale and a year later the Commissioners were complaining to the railway of the poor condition of the canal gates at Highbridge. The B&E replied that its engineer had been instructed to repair the gates.

In 1850 the two parties came into conflict over the control of water levels. The Brue Drainage Act, which governed the actions of the Commissioners, was intended to drain the upper Brue Valley but pen water at lower levels to meet the needs of landowners there. In winter there was plenty of water for both agricultural and canal purposes and the Highbridge clyse gates were normally kept open. In summer their closure achieved the same ends. However keeping the gates closed longer to keep enough water in the canal meant that less use could be made of high tides to scour the mud and prevent the waterway from silting up. This caused a 200yd mudbank to form between the B&E line bridge and the lock gates. At the same time the Commissioners were complaining that slacker holes had been cut in the gates without their authority and that 'the damming up of the river in wet seasons must necessarily entail serious damage to the low-lying lands within the reach of the flood waters of the Brue.'

There were soon complaints that while the drains were empty the canal was full of water. With a duty to maintain sufficient water in the drains for agricultural use, and to prevent damage to waterside land, the Chilton Polden dyke reeves made a presentment about the problem to the Court of Sewers. In turn, the court ordered Highbridge clyse keeper George Wilton to open the gates from 31 October 1850 until the mud in the Brue had been cleared to the dyke reeves' satisfaction. At the same time the clerk to the Commissioners was instructed to write to the B&E asking them to remove the offending mud. The latter, concerned for its newly-purchased asset, responded by asking the Commissioners 'not to let out the water or obstruct the use of the canal' and to call a further meeting to reconsider the order they had made. The railway also asked Commissioner Warry to champion their cause and at a special meeting on 28 November he roundly condemned the folly of the canal own-

The original intention was for the canal and river to join here at Sharpham but an aqueduct and siphon were built instead.

ing element destroying the asset they had just sold, especially as the obstruction was not clearly a railway responsibility.

The chairman of the meeting, Sir Alexander Hood, could see the wisdom of not having to fight both the railway and the lower Brue landowners and prompted a resolution that contained an element of compromise:-

That the clyse keeper be instructed to follow the ancient practice of opening the fresh-water doors; that Messrs. Strangway, Carver and Cripps form a committee, with full powers to make arrangements with the proprietors of the Glastonbury Canal for the removal of obstructions at Highbridge, and expend such sums as they may consider reasonable for the purpose, not exceeding £30.......

The following year seems to have been equally troubled. The clyse gates at Highbridge were reported to be in a poor condition and the B&E had to make further canal repairs. Not that much traffic was now passing but the railway company were still under a statutory obligation to maintain the navigation waterway.

While all this was going on a new development had arisen which was to spell the end of the canal and of its troubles. Seeing no prospect of improvement in the navigation facility, commercial thinking in the area around Glastonbury began to turn to the possibility of a replacement railway. Among the leading supporters of the idea was the expanding footwear business of C & J Clark at Street. Progress was rapid with a public meeting in Glastonbury Town Hall on 16 September 1850 leading to the formation of a steering committee and the commissioning of a route survey. By 21 November 1850 the Somersetshire Central Railway & Highbridge Harbour party was able to give formal notice in the *Bridgwater Times* of its intention to apply to Parliament for powers to make a railway from Highbridge to Glastonbury, to improve Highbridge harbour, and to buy or lease the canal and use it for the route of the new line. Two issues later the new enterprise was inviting share applications.

After more meetings and activity in 1851 the Somerset Central Railway duly secured its enabling Act for 'making a railway from Highbridge to Glastonbury' on 17 June 1852. Of the authorized capital of £70,000, the B&E was to subscribe £10,000 of which £8,000 was to represent the value of the former Glastonbury Canal which the Act allowed the new owners to close and use for their 12 mile 26 chain railway line from Highbridge Wharf to Pasture Field, Glastonbury. The canal formally passed to the Somerset Central undertaking on 16 September 1852.

Work on the new railway began with the cutting of the first sod at Highbridge on 18 April 1853. From beside the wharf the line crossed the B&E route and headed east along the north bank of the River Brue to Cripp's Corner. From there it turned south east towards the South Drain, cutting off the corner created by Cripp's River and the first section of the drain. Still on the north bank, the railway trackbed was laid beside the canal to Ashcott Corner where it changed to the south bank of the navigation to achieve a more direct approach to Glastonbury. The old canal basin there was filled in and became part of the station area.

The Glastonbury Canal enjoyed a brief revival during the railway construction period carrying, ironically, the materials for building the line that was to replace it. Some repairs were even carried out to the bridge and lock at Shapwick. For the year from August 1852 to September 1853 the canal earned £312 of which a large part undoubtedly represent rails, ballast, bridgework and other commodities used in building the line. Expenditure during the same period was £182.

Thanks to being able to use the canal route the new railway was built in just sixteen months although its engineer encountered the same problems in crossing the peat lands east of Shapwick lock that had so troubled the canal company. There was a formal opening on 17 August 1854, when a special train

After the railway crossed the River Brue it took a direct course to Glastonbury compared with that of its canal companion.

ran to Glastonbury for a 'Railway Opening Festival' there, with public services beginning on 28 August. Three months earlier the SCR secretary had been instructed to issue formal closure notices for the canal and it had effectively closed as a through route on 1 July 1854. It seems probable that a few private boat journeys marked its swansong.

At the eastern end of the canal, the waters were drained off and the land level restored on the section between Shapwick Lock and Glastonbury. The lock itself was stripped back to its masonry, along with the Brue and South Drain aqueducts, the work being done by a local man, Thomas Dark of Glastonbury. The bed of the canal was filled in where it was crossed by the route of the Wedmore Turnpike Trust and the various swing bridges became fixed ones. Once the trains were running those portions of the navigation which survived reverted to their drainage function and have continued in that role until the present day. The separate portion of the waterway at the Highbridge end passed to the Commissioners of Sewers and from time to time there have been suggestions of reopening it for scouring purposes but closure and in-filling finally became permanent in 1936.

The Somerset Central Railway, which had cost £80,281 to launch, was leased to the Bristol & Exeter for seven years from the day of opening at a fixed

Shapwick Lock was stripped after closure and its meagre masonry remnants are now buried under a mass of undergrowth.

rental of £3,800 per annum. The SCR kept control of Highbridge Wharf and reduced the tolls operating there to stimulate more traffic. The original route was then extended west to Burnham-on-Sea on 3 May 1858 and east to Wells on 15 March 1859. Three years later a line from Glastonbury to Templecombe was opened to create a link with the Dorset Central Railway. The two companies then amalgamated as the Somerset & Dorset Railway which was soon running coast to coast services and even saw itself as part of a transport route from Wales to France. For many years steamers brought a variety of cargoes into the wharf at Highbridge which had survived the canal closure and flourished in the railway era.

Somerset & Dorset line closures began in the 1950s, with the Highbridge to Glastonbury route finally losing its public train service on 5 March 1966. The short section to the Bason Bridge milk depot and the line to Highbridge Wharf survived until 1972 when the transport part of the Glastonbury Canal story finally ended.

This is the site of the former Somerset & Dorset Railway wharf at Highbridge, formerly the canal basin and with its lock entrance still evident.

ROUTE APPENDIX

One of the major works carried out under the 1801 Brue Drainage Act was the New Cut at Highbridge. Equipped with Higher and Lower Flood Gates to act as main and emergency gates, this new piece of waterway superseded a meandering section of the River Brue and an old clyse (sluice) located where the river crossed under the Bristol road. The plan of the Glastonbury Navigation & Canal was to excavate, straighten and reopen the old route and provide it with a ship basin at the western end and a lock at the road bridge end. Unfortunately the sea basin aspect fell victim to rising costs resulting in tidal restrictions on the western approaches to the waterway, but the fresh-water lock was duly built at the eastern end, although not without difficulties. A 1910 plan shows it as 64ft long, 18ft wide and with 24ft between the sea and freshwater doors. The latter were replaced by a stone sluice before eventual infilling.

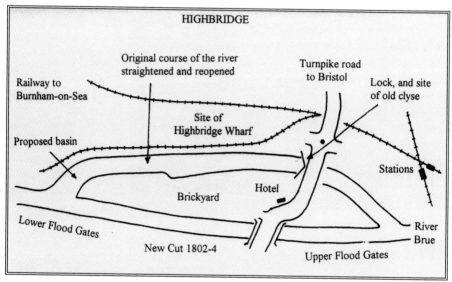

The area that became the Somerset & Dorset Railway's Highbridge Wharf is now largely covered by housing but beyond it is still possible to make out the entrance used by the Glastonbury Canal at Ordnance Survey reference ST474313. Further inland, where the main road passes Jubilee Gardens, the lock entrance can be seen from the area behind the Highbridge Hotel and the waterway route is discernible beyond a brick parapet on the opposite site of the road at ST472318. Nearby Island House marks the fact that the two courses of the Brue did, in fact, create an island.

From Highbridge the route of the river passes beneath the surviving railway and beside the site of the former S&D station and works. It heads off south south east, past the old station and milk factory at Bason Bridge, to its parting with the canal route at Cripp's Bridge, ST452362. The meandering first part of this next Cripp's River section is, in fact, part of a former loop of the Brue which was replaced by a cut-off under the 1801 Act, but the second half is an older waterway probably straightened as part of the outlet for the South Drain. Curiously, some older OS maps show a lock at the northern end of the Cripp's River section and there are suggestions that largish vessels used to travel this far along the lower reaches of the Brue.

A double junction of Cripp's River and South Drain is made at Gold Corner, ST431367 after the former has passed under Little Moor and Eastern Moor bridges. Two more bridges follow before the South Drain is crossed by the route of the S&D Bridgwater branch just before reaching the site of the junction with the Highbridge line and Edington Burtle station at ST428392. Heading on beneath Catcott Bridge the railway trackbed is on the north side of the drainage channel and so continues to Shapwick Lock on the western edge of Westhay Heath. The lock at ST419412 was the beginning of the upper pound of the Glastonbury Canal and some masonry fragments still survive beneath a great deal of undergrowth. Here its usurping railway successor bridged the South Drain to use a route between the two waterways, continuing this way through Shapwick station where it crossed the former Wedmore turnpike road.

The route is now well into peat country and, because of peat workings, the course of the canal would be impossible to trace were it not for the old railway foundations. Further on and still south of its railway companion, the canal is marked by a line of trees in a hollow as its passes the site of Ashcott & Meare station at ST396450. A little further along the twin canal and railway routes the South Drain turns off towards the Polden Hills but still reveals the abutments of the small aqueduct by which it was crossed by the canal on its eastward journey. Beyond this point the railway route changed to the south side of its canal predecessor and stayed that way, past the peat sidings and on to the point where both crossed the River Brue at Sharpham. Here, at ST392480, the original canal intentions had involved either a double lock or an open junction to allow water traffic to follow the river to Pomparles Bridge. In the end an

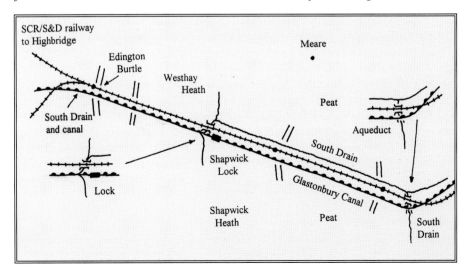

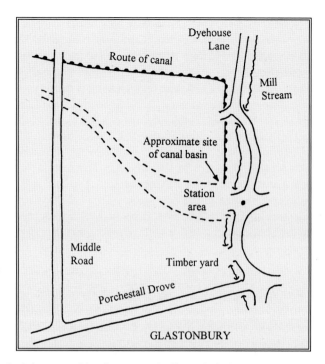

aqueduct and siphon combination were built and their masonry remains are still apparent beside the surviving railway bridge.

The Glastonbury Canal's approach to its home town is today marked only by a narrow drainage ditch, a curved boundary fence and some residual masonry blocks on the western side of Dyehouse Lane at ST392486. Here the waterway apparently made a 90 degree turn south to parallel the road and adjacent Mill Stream on the western side of the historic town. Some plans show a canal basin before the turn was made and Rennie is on record as suggesting that the curve be eased but this did not happen and barges needed to round the awkward corner and continue a little further south to reached the actual canal basin and its buildings.

The site of the basin of the Glastonbury Canal has variously been described as 'north of the railway' and 'near Snow's timber yard' but its exact location is not clear. Where the Mill Stream crosses under Dyehouse Lane a works entrance does reveal a north-south section of ground at a lower level than its surrounds and it seems likely that this was the route of the canal and that the canal basin lay between this depression and the new railway-style gates that have been erected at the entrance to the old station area.

ACKNOWLEDGEMENTS & BIBLIOGRAPHY

The surviving information on the Glastonbury Canal is far from compre-
hensive but in its gathering together a great deal of assistance has been afford-
ed to the authors by the staff of the Somerset Record Office and by David
Bromwich of the Somerset Studies Library. Many others have provided gen-
erous help and encouragement including David Walker of the Somerset Rural
Life Museum and the reference staff of the local libraries at Bridgwater,
Burnham-on-Sea, Glastonbury and Street.

The history of the canal was studied in detail by Dr A.M.Boyd and present-
ed in his paper *The Glastonbury Navigation & Canal 1827-63.* This was
expanded in a subsequent article in the *Journal of the Railway & Canal
Historical Society* and both are essential reading. The subject is well summa-
rized in Charles Hadfield's *The Canals of South West England* (D&C 1985)
and Robin Atthill provided relevant information in an article in Country Life
(June 1967) and in his book *The Somerset & Dorset Railway* (D&C 1985).
The Rev. Richard Warner's 1826 history of Glastonbury echoes the canal
prospectus and Michael William's *The Draining of the Somerset Levels* (CUP
1970) provides essential background information.

Further information is given in the relevant Acts of Parliament, the Rennie
reports, the Somerset River Board papers, the canal prospectus and the contemporary local newspapers of the 1824-54 period.

The etching of the Glastonbury Canal Opening Day is produced by kind per-
mission of the Somerset Archaeological and Natural History Society. Also
included are reproductions from *Woodcuts by Thomas Bewick and his School,*
(edited by Blanche Cirker, published by Dover Publications Inc. New York
1962). All other illustrations have been provided by the authors.

Other titles by FIDUCIA PRESS :

Tom Lamb
The Organ Grinder A verbal obsession   £3.00
Manly Monodes 26 alliterative poems by the Scottish poet   £3.00

Ken Griffiths and Roy Gallop
Fussells Ironworks, Mells (New Edition)   £5.00

Mark Griffiths
Tracts from the Tracks The Ridgeway poems (New Edition)   £5.00

Ernest Clifford Hazell
The Gentle Giants
Shire horses and the history of a timber hauling family 1880-1935   £3.00

Dave Collett
The Dave Collett Blues   A selection of his words and music   £5.00

Dennis Spear
Recollections of Chew Magna A decade to remember 1930-1940   £5.00

Dave Hibberd
Recollections of Jazz in Bristol A rich slice of musical social history   £10.00

Fiducia Press orders and enquires to:
35, Stackpool Road, Southville, Bristol, BS3 1NG.

Titles by **AvonAngliA** include:

Thomas A. Walker
The Severn Tunnel Its construction and difficulties (1872- 1887)   £19.95

Geoffrey Body
Exploring the smaller Towns of Somerset   £6.95

Stephanie Cole
A Passionate Life   The autobiography of a remarkable actor   £9.99

AvonAngliA orders and enquiries to:
74, Ryder Street, Pontcanna, Cardiff, CF11 9BU.